WORLD OF
REPTILES

SEA TURTLES

by Sophie Lockwood

Content Adviser: Harold K. Voris, PhD, Curator and Head,
Amphibians and Reptiles, Department of Zoology,
The Field Museum, Chicago, Illinois

THE CHILD'S WORLD®, CHANHASSEN, MINNESOTA

SEA TURTLES

Published in the United States of America by The Child's World®
PO Box 326 • Chanhassen, MN 55317-0326 • 800-599-READ • www.childsworld.com

Acknowledgements:

The Child's World®: Mary Berendes, Publishing Director

Editorial Directions, Inc.: E. Russell Primm, Editorial Director; Pam Rosenberg, Editor; Judith Shiffer, Assistant Editor; Caroline Wood and Rory Mabin, Editorial Assistants; Susan Hindman, Copy Editor; Emily Dolbear and Sarah E. De Capua, Proofreaders; Elizabeth Nellums, Olivia Nellums, and Daisy Porter, Fact Checkers; Tim Griffin/ IndexServ, Indexer; Cian Loughlin O'Day, Photo Researcher, Linda S. Koutris, Photo Editor

The Design Lab: Kathleen Petelinsek, Art Director, Cartographer; Julia Goozen, Page Production Artist

Photos:

Cover/2-3: Stephen Frink / Digital Vision / Getty Images; frontispiece / 4: Corbis.

Interior: Alamy Images: 11 (Kelvin Aitken / Peter Arnold Inc.), 12 (Michael Patrick O'Neill), 32 (David Schrichte / Photo Resource Hawaii); Animals Animals / Earth Scenes: 5-top left and 8 (OSF / Oliver Grunewald), 29 (Mickey Gibson), 31 (C. C. Lockwood); Corbis: 5-top right and 15 (DiMaggio / Kalish), 5-middle and 21 (William Luther / San Antonio Express-News / ZUMA), 5-bottom right and 27 (Jack Fields), 24 (Connie Rica); Reuters / Corbis: 5-bottom left and 34, 22; Kevin Schaefer / Corbis: 16, 19; Arthur Tilley / Taxi / Getty Images: 36.

Library of Congress Cataloging-in-Publication Data

Lockwood, Sophie.
  Sea turtles / by Sophie Lockwood.
     p. cm. — (The world of reptiles)
  Includes bibliographical references (p.   ) and index.
  ISBN 1-59296-550-4 (library bound : alk. paper)
 1. Sea turtles—Juvenile literature.
 I. Title.
  QL666.C536L634 2006
  597.92'8—dc22   2005024792

TABLE OF CONTENTS

Chapter One

The Sargasso Sea

A desperate journey begins as a sea turtle **hatchling** breaks through its eggshell late at night. The hatchling is a perfect, miniature version of a full-grown turtle. It fits easily in the palm of a human hand.

As the hatchling emerges on the beach, it begins a race for its life. Can the hatchling reach the ocean before being eaten by a gull, crab, or heron? He scurries over the sand along with thousands of other hatchlings. If he is lucky, he will be one of about fifty hatchlings out of every thousand that make it into the water.

Our hatchling reaches the surf. He dives into the water. Minutes-old sea turtles are good swimmers —despite their small size. The hatchling swims rapidly for twenty-four to forty-eight hours. Where is he going in such a hurry?

Instinct leads many sea turtles to a safe place in the open ocean—the Sargasso Sea. This is no ordinary sea. It has no borders and no coastline. It is the size of Australia and located south

Did You Know?
A group of eggs that hatch at one time is called a clutch. Most sea turtle species lay clutches of more than one hundred eggs. During a single season, the female may lay several clutches. With luck, two hatchlings out of each clutch will reach adulthood.

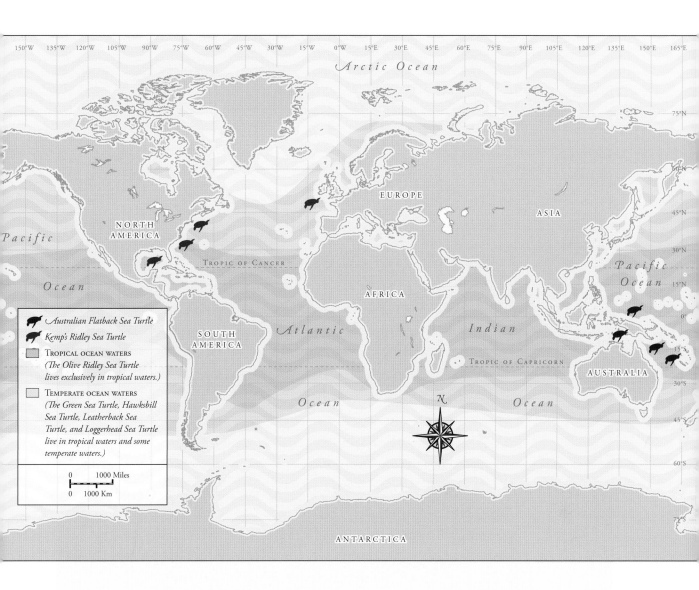

Arctic Ocean

75°N

60°N

EUROPE

ASIA

45°N

Pacific

NORTH
AMERICA

30°N

Ocean

TROPIC OF CANCER

Pacific

Ocean

15°N

AFRICA

0°

SOUTH
AMERICA

Atlantic

Indian

15°S

TROPIC OF CAPRICORN

AUSTRALIA

30°S

Ocean

Ocean

Ocean

45°S

60°S

72°S

ANTARCTICA

🐢 *Australian Flatback Sea Turtle*
🐢 *Kemp's Ridley Sea Turtle*
▢ TROPICAL OCEAN WATERS
(*The Olive Ridley Sea Turtle lives exclusively in tropical waters.*)
▢ TEMPERATE OCEAN WATERS
(*The Green Sea Turtle, Hawksbill Sea Turtle, Leatherback Sea Turtle, and Loggerhead Sea Turtle live in tropical waters and some temperate waters.*)

0   1000 Miles
0   1000 Km

of Bermuda. The Gulf Stream runs to the west of this
strange sea. The Greater Antilles marks the south. The
sea—a body of warm, calm, clear water—churns in a
slow clockwise motion.

This map shows the range of sea turtle habitats.

Baby leatherback sea turtles emerge from their nest and begin their dangerous journey to the ocean.

The Sargasso Sea creates a remarkable **ecosystem.** Algae and bladder wrack are among the seaweeds that bob on the open ocean. The most common seaweed there is the yellow-brown sargassum. Its air-filled bladders keep it afloat in any weather.

Seaweeds provide food for the ocean's plant eaters. The smallest plant life is so tiny, it must be seen through a microscope. Animals that are nearly as small eat the tiny plants. In turn, those animals are food for crabs, shrimp, jellyfish, and Portuguese men-of-war. Strangely, freshwater eels from Europe and North America gather at the Sargasso Sea to lay their eggs. The millions of eel eggs also provide food for the creatures grazing in the seaweed network.

The hatchling makes it. He swam hundreds of miles. He dove deep to avoid hungry seabirds. He steered clear of large fish that also prey on turtles. Now he moves into the Sargasso Sea. How long he will live there no one knows.

Most sea turtle species feast on the buffet supplied by the Sargasso Sea. Different species have different diets. There is plenty for all. Baby turtles must grow to dinner-

plate size—about 12 inches (30 centimeters) long—before they are safe from most **predators.**

Our hatchling is a baby leatherback turtle. His species gets its name from its upper shell, which is made of tough, rubbery, leatherlike skin. Leatherbacks feed mostly on jellyfish. There are many species of jellyfish in the ocean, so, fortunately, leatherbacks usually have plenty of food.

The young leatherback will grow to be enormous. Sea turtles are measured by the size of their upper shells. They can measure 4 to 8 feet (1.2 to 2.4 meters) long and weigh, at most, about 1,300 pounds (590 kilograms). If the hatchling reaches this size, few predators will attack him. Only orcas prey on adult leatherbacks.

Leatherbacks may swim as far north as Greenland or Alaska. They may travel around the cape in Africa. Still their futures are unknown. It is likely that only human protection can ensure the survival of leatherbacks and all other sea turtle species.

Did You Know?
Little is known about the lives of male sea turtles because they rarely return to land. Scientists count sea turtle species populations by the number of nesting females. The number of males, nonbreeding females, or young of both sexes is unknown. Kemp's ridley sea turtles have the smallest population—about 1,000 nesting females.

A leatherback sea turtle returns to the water. Adult female sea turtles come ashore to nest, but adult males rarely, if ever, leave the water.

Chapter Two

Shells and Bills

Sea turtles belong to the Testudines group, which includes turtles and tortoises. They are related to snapping turtles, pond turtles, desert tortoises, and gigantic Galápagos tortoises. The first turtles appeared 245 million to 208 million years ago. Scientists have found fossils of early sea turtles from 208 million to 144 million years ago. Many animal species evolved and disappeared while sea turtles thrived in the seas. Turtles have outlasted dinosaurs, woolly mammoths, and hundreds of other species.

There are seven species of sea turtles: Australian flatback, green, hawksbill, leatherback, loggerhead, Kemp's ridley, and olive ridley. Some scientists consider the black turtle, a subspecies of green sea turtles, as another separate sea turtle species.

Sea turtles are reptiles. Like all reptiles, they are cold-blooded. This means they have no internal control of their body temperature. A sea turtle's body temperature is nearly the same as the temperature of the water it swims in. For that reason, most sea turtles live in tropical waters.

The hawksbill sea turtle is found in tropical and subtropical waters.

The most outstanding feature of every sea turtle is its shell. The top section of the shell is called the carapace. The bony scales on most species' carapaces are called scutes. They look like—and are—turtle armor. The lower shell is called a plastron. For most sea turtles, the carapace is dark colored and patterned. The plastron is pale colored, from white to yellow or beige. A bony bridge holds the carapace and plastron together.

Sea turtles have no teeth. Their mouths and snouts are sometimes called bills. Leatherbacks usually limit their eating to jellyfish. Adult green sea turtles munch only on sea grasses. Other species of sea turtle, however, manage to crunch on clams, shrimp, crabs, and mussels.

REPRODUCTION

Sea turtles lay eggs, just like chickens. Females return to the same beach where they were born to dig their nests. They return to their birthplaces by instinct. They drag their heavy bodies over the sand, just as their mothers, grandmothers, and great-grandmothers did in the past.

The hawksbill's beautiful shell is prized by humans. Though it is illegal, in many places
the turtles are killed so that their shells can be made into jewelry and other items.

Kemp's ridley sea turtles nest at only one beach at Rancho Nuevo, Mexico. Their arrival is called an *arribada*. All the turtles arrive at nearly the same time and lay their eggs in nests. Female Kemp's ridleys deposit about 110 eggs into their nests, then cover them with sand. Kemp's ridleys lay between one and four clutches of eggs yearly.

A female green turtle creates a nest on Ascension Island in the South Atlantic.

Most other sea turtle species lay eggs every two, three, or more years. Loggerheads lay the most eggs per nesting season: up to seven nests a year with between 100 and 126 eggs per nest. Hawksbills lay the most eggs per nest, about 160. Australian flatbacks lay the fewest eggs per nest—only fifty at a time. While this may seem like a huge number of eggs, the probability of an egg becoming an adult sea turtle is very small. Raccoons, dogs, and other predators gorge themselves on eggs. And only about one out of a thousand hatchlings reach adulthood.

Most female sea turtles reproduce for the first time when they are between ten and twenty-five years old. If a sea turtle makes it to adulthood, it lives a long life. How long? The life span of sea turtles is still being studied. Loggerheads may live sixty to seventy-five years or longer. Green sea turtles live up to eighty-five years. It is difficult, however, to determine the age of a turtle. So, like many other details about sea turtles, no one really knows.

Australian Flatback Sea Turtle Fast Facts
(Natator depressa)
Adult length: Up to 39 inches (99 cm)
Weight: About 198 pounds (90 kg)
Coloration: Olive-gray carapace with brown or yellow on edges, white flippers
Range: Coastal waters of northern Australia, Gulf of Papua New Guinea
Breeding: 4 nests per season, 50 eggs per nest
Diet: Sea cucumbers, jellyfish, mollusks, and shrimp
U.S. status: Not enough data to determine

Chapter Three

Tracking Turtles

For hundreds of years, people have had no idea what happened to sea turtles once they hatched. Even today, after years of scientific effort, there's plenty we still don't know.

Since the 1970s, scientists have realized that some sea turtle species were in danger of becoming **extinct.** Today, the sea turtle species with the largest population is the olive ridley, with about 800,000 nesting females. But olive ridleys look so much like the critically endangered Kemp's ridley that **conservation** organizations have listed olive ridleys as endangered, to protect the Kemp's from hunters.

What happens to sea turtles once they reach the open ocean? We don't know. Scientists have no idea how long hatchlings stay at their first site. They call this first year the "lost year." Scientists believe young turtles float around in the ocean until they are large enough to sur-

Kemp's Ridley Sea Turtle Fast Facts
(Lepidochelys kempi)
Adult length: 24 to 28 inches (62 to 70 cm)
Weight: 77 to 100 pounds (35 to 45 kg)
Coloration: Dark, gray-green carapace with a white or yellowish plastron
Range: Gulf of Mexico, occasionally north to New England and east to Great Britain and Europe
Breeding: Nesting season yearly, 2 nests per season, average of 110 eggs per nest
Diet: Crabs, clams, mussels, shrimp, fish, sea urchins, squid, and jellyfish
U.S. status: Critically endangered

Olive ridley sea turtles, such as this one in Costa Rica, look a lot like Kemp's ridley sea turtles.

vive. Some **juveniles** may follow certain ocean currents and move near the seashore where food is plentiful.

Scientists use modern technology to find answers to age-old questions. Radio beacons and satellite tracking let scientists follow adult sea turtles on their strange, mysterious voyages.

Several different research groups track sea turtles. They catch a turtle, glue on a radio transmitter, and track the animal by satellite. Catching the turtles takes place when females are on nesting beaches or when males are spotted swimming near nesting beaches.

The Caribbean Conservation Corporation and the Sea Turtle Survival League pay for many turtle tracking programs. The Georgia Loggerhead Tracking Project follows a number of females throughout the year. The females were captured after laying their eggs. One subject, named Cherokee Rose, is one of the largest turtles studied in this project. Cherokee Rose measures 40 inches (102 centimeters) long.

The Tampa Bay tracking program caught and

Did You Know?

Green sea turtles, once their carapace reaches about 10 inches (25 cm), eat only sea grasses that grow in coastal shallows. They are the only adult sea turtles that are herbivores.

A Kemp's ridley sea turtle is released on the Padre Island Seashore. Scientists attached a satellite transmitter to the turtle and will be able to track its movements.

Volunteers in Honduras measure a leatherback sea turtle that has come ashore to nest.

tagged several leatherback males at sea. The tracking showed leatherbacks feed along the shallows of Florida's west coast. Occasionally, they take side trips deeper into the Gulf of Mexico.

Why track turtles? All sea turtles are either threatened or endangered in the wild. The only way to build an intelligent, effective conservation plan is to know how turtles live. By tracking them, scientists plot when and where turtles travel. Popular migration routes can be protected from net fishing. Already, laws safeguard nesting sites throughout the world. The next step is to protect these mysterious creatures in the open sea.

Loggerhead Sea Turtle Fast Facts
(Caretta caretta)
Adult length: 30 to 42 inches (76 to 107 cm)
Weight: Up to 350 pounds (159 kg)
Coloration: Reddish-brown carapace with yellowish plastron
Range: Temperate and tropical waters worldwide
Breeding: Nesting season every 2 or more years, 4 to 7 nests, averages between 100 and 126 eggs per nest
Diet: Horseshoe crabs, clams, mussels, and invertebrates
U.S. status: Threatened

Chapter Four

Turtle Folklore

Long ago, native people of North America called Earth "Turtle Island." They passed on the **creation myth** of Sky Woman and the Great Turtle:

Long ago, before man walked the Earth, a man in Heaven pulled up a great tree. This left a huge hole, which his wife looked through. She leaned over and fell into the hole and left the Heavens.

Far below, winged creatures swam the open seas. The creatures saw Sky Woman falling and hurried to catch her. The creatures brought Sky Woman to the Great Turtle, who was also swimming the ocean.

Many creatures tried to bring mud from beneath the ocean to build a land home for Sky Woman. None succeeded. Finally, Muskrat brought up mud and coated the Great Turtle's shell. Sky Woman went to sleep, and during the night the Great Turtle's back grew larger. Streams, grass, trees, and plants grew. The turtle's back became the land on which humans live.

An American Indian storyteller tells a tale in Saint Charles, Missouri.

Did You Know?
In Iroquois folklore, the Great Turtle is considered to be the wisest of all creatures.

Green Sea Turtle Fast Facts
(Chelonia mydas)
Adult length: More than 3 feet (1 m)
Weight: 300 to 350 pounds (136 to 159 kg)
Coloration: Light to dark green carapace with white or yellow plastron
Range: Temperate and tropical waters worldwide
Breeding: Nesting season every 2 or more years, 3 to 5 nests, 115 eggs per nest
Diet: Turtles up to about 10 inches (25 cm) eat worms, insects, grasses, and crustaceans; turtles more than 10 inches (25 cm) eat sea grasses and algae
U.S. status: Endangered

Native Hawaiians called their turtle goddess Kauila. She was a sea turtle born when her parents, two magical turtle spirits, laid a single egg in the black sands of Hawaii. After her birth, Kauila and her mother dug a deep, freshwater pond where Hawaiian children drank and swam in safety.

Many cultures honored the sea turtle. In the Miskito Cays, islands off Nicaragua, the native people still tell stories of the Turtle Mother.

Chinese, Greek, and Egyptian traditions considered sea turtles sacred. Thailand natives chose the turtles as a symbol of endless life. The Aztecs of ancient Mexico believed the turtle represented a coward or a boaster. The Aborigines of Australia consider the turtle an important part of their heritage.

TURTLES AND ART

Early cultures depicted sea turtles in many ways. Ancient cave and stone paintings draw the sea turtle's shape in browns, white, and yellows. The Moche of Peru (200 B.C. to A.D. 700) made pottery cups, bowls, and jars in the shape of many animals, including sea turtles. Natives of southwestern Florida made ritual masks in the shape of a hawksbill turtle's head. The use for those masks is unknown.

Carved wooden hangings, jewelry, and tattoos draw the interest of native people and tourists alike in Hawaii and other Pacific Islands. And, for more practical artwork, dozens of stamps graced with pictures of sea turtles have gone on sale in Papua New Guinea, Trinidad, Christmas Island, and, surprisingly, Yugoslavia.

Ancient residents of Hawaii created this stone carving, or petroglyph, of a sea turtle.

Chapter Five

Humans and Sea Turtles

For centuries, humans hunted sea turtles. They captured nesting females and collected turtle eggs. Turtle meat ended up in the stew pot. Turtle oil lit lamps in the night. The skin became drumheads, shoes, and belts. Shells were made into jewelry or used whole as bowls. But native hunters took only the turtles they needed to survive. Turtle populations continued to thrive.

Unfortunately, large-scale hunting of turtles at nesting sites has been the number-one killer of adult sea turtles by humans. Eggs were also harvested in large numbers. In addition, large fishing boats often accidentally catch sea turtles.

Today, hunting sea turtles breaks both U.S. and international laws. Unfortunately, illegal hunting continues. In particular, green, olive ridley, and hawksbill turtles are taken for their beautiful shells. Turtle shells are used

to make jewelry and tortoiseshell eyeglass frames. Native people have permission for **subsistence hunting.** They need the meat for food.

THREATS TO SURVIVAL

Sea turtles face many threats to their survival. Natural threats are a normal part of life. Storms wash away nests

It is against the law to kill sea turtles for their shells, but they are still sold in some places such as these for sale in Indonesia.

or batter beaches where females would normally dig nests. Raccoons, dogs, crabs, and wolves prey on eggs. Birds and fish feast on hatchlings as they make their way to the open ocean. This is part of our natural system and does not bring a species to near extinction. It is human activity that has endangered the sea turtle species.

Fishing and shrimp trawling once accounted for more than fifty thousand sea turtle deaths each year. Ships dragged huge nets behind their ships, often catching more than the fish they sought. Sea turtles breathe air. When caught in nets, the turtles drowned. Today, U.S. fishing nets are required to have TEDS, turtle elimination devices. Although some fisheries in other countries refuse to use nets with TEDS, most do. TEDS have saved many thousands of turtles.

Pollution is another problem threatening sea turtles. Plastic is particularly dangerous. Plastic bags and balloons look a lot like jellyfish—a popular dish among sea turtles. Sea turtles eat the

Hawksbill Sea Turtle Fast Facts
(Eretmochelys imbricata)
Adult length: 30 to 36 inches (76 to 91 cm)
Weight: 100 to 150 pounds (45 to 68 kg)
Coloration: Orange, brown, or yellow carapace
Range: Tropical and subtropical waters worldwide
Breeding: Nesting season every 2 or more years, 2 to 4 nests, 160 eggs per nest
Diet: Sponges, anemones, squid, and shrimp
U.S. status: Endangered

Sea turtles, like other reptiles, breathe air. Those caught in fishing nets, such as this loggerhead, will drown because they won't be able to get to the ocean surface to breathe.

What You Can Do
Whenever you go to the
beach, pick up any garbage
you make or see and
put it in a trash can. Be
particularly careful about
plastics, as they cause the
most harm to sea turtles.

plastic but cannot digest it. The plastic sits in a turtle's stomach, and the turtle never feels hungry. It starves to death because of a carelessly discarded grocery bag.

Nesting sites create different problems. The beaches where sea turtles traditionally nest have become resorts filled with condos, parking lots, and restaurants. Bright

A green sea turtle walks on the beach in Hawaii. Improvements that make beaches better for human tourists don't necessarily benefit sea turtles.

lights attract turtle hatchlings and confuse them. Instead of heading to the water, hatchlings head to fast-food parking lots. There they get picked off by birds or other animals, or they die from lack of food and water.

Beach "improvements" do not improve life for nesting female turtles. Humans try to thwart the waves and tides by armoring the beach. They build seawalls, breakwaters, and jetties, which block female turtles trying to reach their nesting beach. Sometimes, beaches are "nourished." People add new sand to make a prettier, smoother beach. Unless this sand is similar in texture to the original sand, nesting females may become confused and fail to dig nests. The answers to these problems are simple: leave the beaches and turtles to Mother Nature.

CONSERVATION GOALS

Several conservation groups work to protect sea turtles from extinction. These groups and others have several goals, which play a part in the survival plan of sea turtles. A major goal is to ensure that hatchlings reach adulthood. In some cases, to do so requires human interference. Scientists collect and incubate turtle eggs in nurseries. Humans raise hatchlings until they reach dinner-plate size, which is the size at which they are safe

from most predators. It is hoped that this technique will help Kemp's ridley turtles recover their population.

Another goal is to stop illegal trade in sea turtle meat, leather, and shells. It is against the law to bring turtle items into the United States. The penalty for doing so may be as high as a $20,000 fine and a year in jail. Unfortunately, catching the criminals is difficult.

A baby sea turtle is prepared for its return to the sea in Thailand. Conservation groups throughout the world are working to save sea turtles from extinction.

The use of TEDs on fishing nets has reduced the number of turtles caught by nets. But it is important to enforce the use of TEDs by all shrimp trawlers and fishing ships. Protecting nesting and feeding sites will also help increase the sea turtle population.

Sea turtle conservation news is positive. One great success story is Tortuguero, Costa Rica. There a 22-mile (35-kilometer) stretch of beach provides the most important nesting site for green sea turtles in the Western Hemisphere. In the 1960s, locals made their living by catching female turtles for their meat and harvesting turtle eggs. Since then, residents have found hosting tourists much more profitable.

In the 1960s, about twenty thousand nesting females came ashore at Tortuguero. Today, that number is more than fifty thousand. This is not a guarantee that all is well, however. Because green turtles must reach at least twenty-five years old before being able to produce young, it may be several more years before scientists can be sure the green turtle population is healthy.

Kemp's ridleys, the most endangered sea turtles, owe their survival in part to the Padre Island National Seashore, Texas. This facility is part of the National Park Service and has an active sea turtle science and recovery program.

Participating in beach cleanups can help save sea turtles and other animals that depend on seashore habitats for survival.

The team hopes to reestablish a nesting colony on the island. Similar projects are at work in Florida, Bermuda, Barbados, and Mexico.

Educating people about sea turtles and their problems helps control the threats that reduce sea turtle populations. Humans can help save sea turtles. Classes and individuals can adopt sea turtles from afar and then follow the paths of their turtles online. People can take part in beach cleanup programs. Along the coastline where nesting sites exist, restaurants, stores, and families can turn off their outside lights at night so that hatchlings head immediately to the surf instead of the parking lots.

Every individual can do small things that save sea turtles. In the end, those acts add up to species survival. And not just for sea turtles. Every endangered species can be saved with a bit of help from all of us.

Glossary

carapace (KAR-uh-payss) a turtle's upper shell

conservation (kon-sur-VAY-shuhn) the act of saving or preserving some aspect of wildlife

creation myth (kree-AY-shuhn MITH) a story about how the world began

ecosystem (EE-koh-siss-tuhm) all the plants, animals, and physical features in which a species lives

endangered (ehn-DAYN-jurd) threatened with extinction

extinct (ek-STINGKT) no longer existing

hatchling (HACH-ling) an animal newly emerged from an egg

instinct (IN-stingkt) one's natural sense of what is happening with one's body or actions one takes

juveniles (JOO-vuh-nuhlz) youngsters, like human toddlers

plastron (PLASS-truhn) a turtle's lower shell

pollution (puh-LOO-shuhn) the fouling of air, water, or land by waste, chemicals, or other contaminating agents

predators (PRED-uh-turz) animals that hunt and kill other animals for food

subsistence hunting (suhb-SISS-tuhns HUNT-ing) hunting just enough to maintain life

threatened (THRET-uhnd) a state of approaching extinction

For More Information

Watch It

Sea Turtles: Ancient Nomads. VHS (New York: National Audubon Society, 1994).

Wildlife Survivors: Tale of Two Turtles & Dolphins in Danger. DVD (Reston, Va., National Wildlife Federation, produced by Madacy Entertainment Group, 2004).

Read It

Cerullo, Mary M. *Sea Turtles: Ocean Nomads.* New York: Dutton's Children's Books, 2003.

Kalman, Bobbie. *Endangered Sea Turtles.* New York: Crabtree Publishing Company, 2004.

Look It Up

Visit our home page for lots of links about sea turtles: *http://www.childsworld.com/links*

Note to Parents, Teachers, and Librarians: We routinely verify our Web links to make sure they are safe, active sites—so encourage your readers to check them out!

The Animal Kingdom
Where Do Sea Turtles Fit In?

Kingdom: Animal

Phylum: Chordata

Class: Reptilia

Order: Testudines (turtles and tortoises)

Family: Cheloniidae or Dermochelyidae

Genus and Species:
Caretta caretta—loggerhead
Chelonia mydas—green
Dermochelys coriacea— leatherback
Eretmochelys imbricata— hawksbill
Lepidochelys kempi—Kemp's ridley
Lepidochelys olivacea—olive ridley
Natator depressa—Australian flatback

Index

About the Author

Sophie Lockwood is a former teacher and a longtime writer. She writes textbooks, newspaper articles, and magazine articles. Sophie enjoys writing about animals and their habits. The most interesting part of her research, Sophie says, is learning how scientists apply their knowledge to save endangered species. She lives with her husband in the foothills of the Blue Ridge Mountains.